U.S. Department of Justice
Bureau of Alcohol, Tobacco, Firearms and Explosives

I0448530

Violent Crime Impact Teams

Best Practices

Foreword by the Director

Gun violence negatively impacts our families and our communities, and the Bureau of Alcohol, Tobacco, Firearms and Explosives (ATF) is the Federal agency charged with reducing gun violence. In June 2004, the Department of Justice (DOJ) and ATF designed the Violent Crime Impact Team (VCIT) initiative to identify, arrest, and prosecute those offenders responsible for crippling our communities. The VCIT initiative was developed and initially deployed as a 6-month pilot program in 15 cities.

An evaluation of the program reveals significant successes. During the 6-month pilot period, 13 out of the 15 VCIT areas reported decreases in homicides committed with firearms, as compared to the same period the previous year. In total, VCIT areas witnessed a 17 percent decline in homicides committed with guns.

The VCIT program emphasizes the importance of using the information we handle while focusing our resources. Over the past decade, investigators have benefited from an enormous increase in the access to information. Presently, ATF's National Tracing Center has collected over one million traces of firearms recovered by law enforcement officials in our firearms trafficking information system. The National Integrated Ballistic Information Network (NIBIN) contains ballistic images of over 900,000 pieces of evidence, which have generated investigative leads that may not have been realized without such technology. These advances in the tools used to access and analyze investigative information enable ATF and our Federal, State and local partners to identify many more criminals, and to evaluate and respond to specific local crime patterns. Yet success in combating violent firearms crime lies in much more than technology. Success is a result of teamwork and the integration of local intelligence, knowledge, and skills, with full use of the investigative resources brought to the table by ATF and our partners.

This Best Practices report identifies the specific practices that contributed most to the pilot program's success, and this analysis will be used to strengthen future VCIT deployments. The evidence presented in this report also illustrates how much can be achieved through cooperative law enforcement efforts. Through VCIT, ATF and local communities have worked together in partnership to attack the criminal element, helping to bring security and safety back to America's cities. By incorporating lessons learned into future VCIT areas, we will strive to replicate these successes across the Nation.

Carl J. Truscott
Bureau of Alcohol, Tobacco,
Firearms and Explosives

Executive Summary

In June 2004, the Department of Justice (DOJ) and the Bureau of Alcohol, Tobacco, Firearms and Explosives (ATF) announced the deployment of Violent Crime Impact Teams (VCIT) in 15 cities. This pilot program, designed and implemented in collaboration with the Deputy Attorney General, sought to extend recent reductions in the rate of overall violent crime to select areas exhibiting significant numbers of homicides. Fourteen of the fifteen cities selected for the initial deployment of the VCITs saw homicides climb from 1,425 to 1,605 – an increase of 13 percent between 2002 and 2003. (Los Angeles was the only VCIT city that did not realize an increase in homicides.) The VCIT program was designed to identify, target, disrupt, arrest and prosecute the "worst of the worst" criminals responsible for violent crime in identified hot spots, through the use of innovative technologies, analytical investigative resources, and an integrated Federal, State, and local law enforcement strategy.

An evaluation of the program following 6 months of operation revealed significant reductions of homicides in many of the geographic hot spots targeted by VCITs. During the 6-month pilot period, 13 out of the 15 VCIT areas reported decreases in homicides committed with firearms, compared to the same period the previous year. In total, VCIT areas witnessed a 17 percent decline in homicides committed with guns (see Table 1). In the 13 VCIT areas demonstrating success, 138 fewer homicides were committed with firearms compared to the same period the previous year, a 33 percent decline. VCITs contributed to these positive results by arresting more than 500 identified individuals, recovering more than 3,000 firearms, and the seizing more than $2 million. In addition to apprehending targeted offenders, VCIT agents and officers also arrested more than 2,500 gang members, drug dealers, felons in possession of firearms, and other criminals of significance, during the course of VCIT operations.

ATF has reviewed VCIT enforcement strategies as devised and implemented by ATF and Federal, State and local partners, and documented common practices that contributed to its success. The following 10 best practices were identified in after-action surveys and articulated in interviews conducted with VCIT leaders.

1. **Set clear goals and measure performance;**

2. **Develop collaborative partnerships with local police;**

3. **Target the "worst of the worst" criminals;**

4. **Use the full array of intelligence assets;**

5. **Maintain a fluid and dynamic approach when targeting offenders and hot spots;**

6. **Conduct proactive street enforcement with local police in targeted hot spots.**

7. **Deploy resources during peak hours of criminal activity;**

8. **Investigate the sources of firearms linked to violent crime;**

9. **Prioritize prosecution of defendants linked to targeted hot spots; and**

10. **Publicize success stories.**

This document communicates lessons learned and presents recommendations to be considered in conjunction with future VCIT operations.

VIOLENT CRIME IMPACT TEAMS
Homicides with Firearms
Statistical Pilot Performance Assessment

City	2003 Jun-Nov	2004 Jun-Nov	%Change
Albuquerque	4	2	-50%
Baltimore	91	128	41%
Chattanooga	6	2	-67%
Columbus	32	26	-19%
Greensboro	13	3	-77%
Las Vegas	62	51	-18%
Los Angeles	72	77	7%
Miami	36	22	-39%
Pittsburgh	33	13	-61%
Philadelphia	12	3	-75%
Richmond	51	38	-25%
Tampa	19	9	-53%
Tucson	24	18	-25%
Tulsa	29	12	-59%
Washington, DC/Virginia	92	76	-17%
TOTALS	576	480	-17%

Table 1

Note 1: Las Vegas and Philadelphia compare the time period July through December, since the program was initiated in July, 2004.

Note 2: This data is preliminary and is subject to change.

Note 3: Where available, data represents statistics for the target areas within the city identified and not a citywide or metropolitan statistical area.

Background

ATF's analysis of violent crime patterns prompted the Bureau to focus on certain violent crimes. Although overall violent crime rates reached historic lows from 1999 to 2003 (see Graph 1), homicides with firearms began to rise during this same time (see Graph 2), a disturbing trend that the Violent Crime Impact Team (VCIT) program was designed to address.

NATIONAL VIOLENT CRIME LANDSCAPE
Crime Trends Prior to VCIT Implementation
Crime Rates Per 100,000 Population

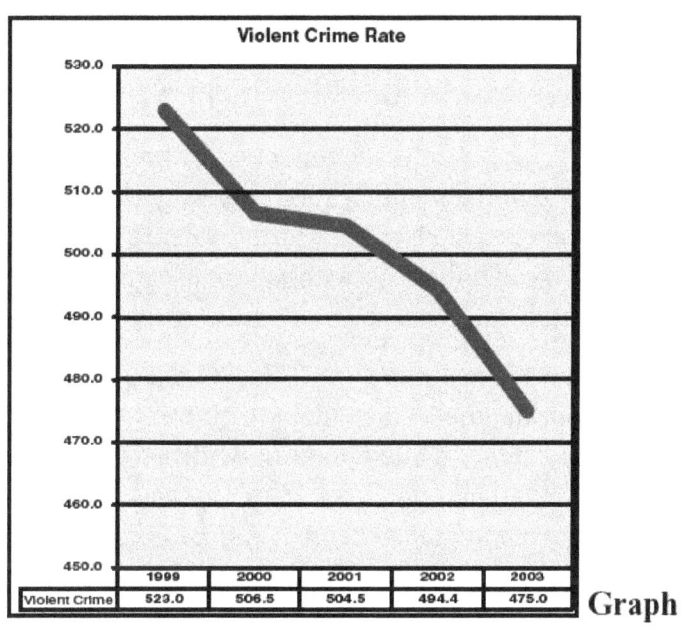

Violent Crime Rate

	1999	2000	2001	2002	2003
Violent Crime	523.0	506.5	504.5	494.4	475.0

Graph 1

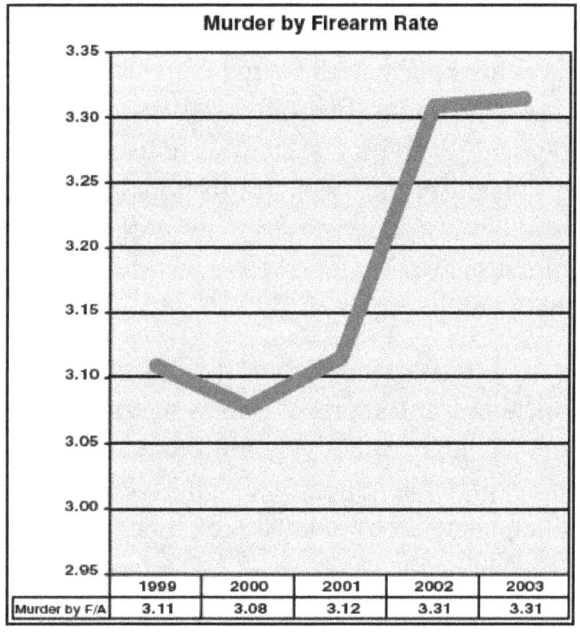

Murder by Firearm Rate

	1999	2000	2001	2002	2003
Murder by F/A	3.11	3.08	3.12	3.31	3.31

Graph 2

In June 2004, the Department of Justice (DOJ) and the Bureau of Alcohol, Tobacco, Firearms and Explosives (ATF) announced the deployment of VCITs in 15 cities. As the lead Federal law enforcement agency in the fight against violent firearms crime, ATF was charged with coordinating the program. The VCIT concept, designed and implemented in collaboration with the Deputy Attorney General, sought to extend recent reductions in the rate of overall violent crime to select areas exhibiting significant numbers of homicides. The foundation of the VCIT program was the identification, targeting, disruption, arrest and prosecution of the "worst of the worst" criminals responsible for violent crime in targeted hot spots. Fundamental to this effort was the use of innovative technologies, analytical investigative resources, and an integrated Federal, State, and local law enforcement strategy.

Goals and Objectives of the Violent Crime Impact Teams

The goal of the VCIT program is the reduction of homicides and other firearms-related violence through the identification, investigation, and arrest of those responsible for violent crime. The long-term measure of the VCIT's success is the mitigation of localized crime without displacement of the violence to neighboring communities.

From the violent street gang activity in Tulsa, Oklahoma, to home invasion crews in Tampa, Florida, the VCITs adapt to address the violent crime problems within the cities they serve, while operating within a programmatic framework that seeks to achieve national goals. In 13 of 15 cities, gangs and their members were linked to increases in violent crime. As a result, localized VCIT tactics became anti-gang strategies in varying degrees.

The VCIT strategy dictates applying technology to identify hot spots and to target, investigate and arrest violent offenders. ATF's National Tracing Center, Crime Gun Analysis Branch, Regional Crime Gun Centers (RCGC), and other technologies, such as the National Integrated Ballistic Information Network (NIBIN) and geographic information systems, are used to pinpoint localized crime problems and to identify the "worst of the worst" criminals. Integrating intelligence from local law enforcement agencies with information produced through new technologies is fundamental to successfully combating violent firearms crime in these neighborhoods.

Through lessons learned from past collaborative efforts, ATF recognized that Federal, State, and local law enforcement efforts to combat violent crime and gang-related problems could be effectively multiplied through an influx of federal resources and experience. Specifically, partnerships developed with community leaders help generate previously untapped resources that can be directed to counter violent crime. As a result, ATF has partnered with social service agencies, nonprofit community assistance agencies, faith-based groups, schools, and private businesses to promote a comprehensive and coordinated community action plan to advance the goals of gang suppression, intervention, and prevention. ATF continues its effort to broadcast success stories to the community through local media. An effective media campaign, publicizing the arrest and severe penalties received by individuals who commit crimes of violence proved to be a strong and convincing deterrent to offenders contemplating future crimes.

VCIT employs traditional means to proactively develop criminal cases. Team members utilize undercover techniques and informants in their work to identify, investigate and seek prosecution against gang members, illicit gun possessors, and firearms traffickers. VCITs obtain Federal and/or State search and arrest warrants in an effort to remove gang members and other violent offenders from the community. Assistant United States Attorneys assigned to the task forces facilitate the timely and efficient handling of Federal court proceedings for offenders referred for prosecution, in concert with counterparts at local District Attorneys' offices.

Team members review and screen each police report that documents firearms-related violence committed within their VCIT's areas of operation, leading to Federal prosecutions of gang members and other violent offenders for firearms violations. When Federal prosecution is not warranted, offenders are, at a minimum, interviewed about their sources of firearms. VCITs work along with gang, robbery, and narcotics units operating in targeted areas. VCIT members are active within targeted hot spots during peak hours of violence and respond immediately following the occurrence of firearms-related crimes.

When responding to firearms-related crime scenes, including homicides, VCIT members assist the local police by investigating all firearms-related leads and ensuring firearms evidence is traced, and when possible, ballistically imaged and queried through NIBIN. In addition, ATF-trained explosives detection canines and canine handlers are made available to VCITs to aid in the recovery of firearms and ballistic evidence from crime scenes and search warrant locations.

Program Implementation Best Practices

BEST PRACTICE # 1: Set clear goals and measure performance.

What gets measured gets done. A combination of output and outcome measures is critical to proper implementation of any enforcement strategy. Daily reinforcement of goals further strengthens group effectiveness. Training and observable changes in the level of dedication by Federal partners solidify the importance of stated goals.

In Albuquerque, New Mexico, the VCIT supervisor met with ATF agents and clearly told his employees that their measure of success would be based solely on a reduction in firearms related violent crime. The VCIT supervisor communicated this same message to patrol officers. He stressed that it would not be business as usual and that his agents would be working side-by-side with officers on the street. The VCIT supervisor also tasked different ATF agents, on a weekly basis, to complete necessary statistical reporting required by ATF Headquarters. This allowed each team member to understand firsthand how the group's performance was being measured.

Finally, the group had to be flexible to the ever-changing flow of informant-based information concerning targeted individuals and shifting hot spots of crime. The VCIT supervisor found it useful to set daily goals and priorities at roll call so the group's efforts were routinely refocused on results every evening of operation.

In the Southeast-area command of Albuquerque, homicides committed with firearms were reduced 50 percent during the 6-month pilot period. Citywide, homicides decreased from 63 in 2003 to 58 in 2004, with a marked drop in gang- and drug-related killings, which fell from 15 in 2003 to 8 in 2004.

BEST PRACTICE # 2: Develop collaborative partnerships with local police.

Networking is crucial in advance of collaborative relationships. The time to develop professional relationships is prior to the creation of task forces, not during the building of such groups. The key to VCIT's success was the combined effort of all parties involved. City police and sheriff's departments, State probation and parole offices; and agents from the Drug Enforcement Administration, the Federal Bureau of Investigation and the United States Marshals Service were fundamental to VCIT's operations and VCIT's impact on violent crime.

The Tulsa VCIT found it necessary for each law enforcement partner to dedicate people to this operation on a full-time basis. Even though ATF's Tulsa Field Office was already working with the Tulsa Police Department (TPD) on addressing gang problems, the renewed commitment and assignment of additional personnel to VCIT showed ATF's willingness to make this project a success. This further strengthened the existing cooperative relationship shared between ATF agents and TPD Officers. Citywide, homicides in Tulsa dropped from 70 in 2003 to 46 in 2004. During the VCIT pilot program, homicides with a firearm dropped from 29 in 2003 to 12 during the same 6-month period in 2004.

BEST PRACTICE # 3: Target the "worst of the worst" criminals.

Identifying the most active and violent offenders and using every available tool to investigate them provided the foundation of the overall success of several VCIT operations. Properly compiling complete lists of those identified with photos, public record information printouts, and current and past arrest information assisted many VCITs in identifying their main targets. Ensuring these identified individuals were incarcerated for any violation, whether it occurred in Federal or State court, reduced the chance of another shooting within the targeted area. While many of the identified offenders were arrested on individual charges such as Possession of a Firearm by a Felon, Dealing Narcotics While Armed, or Possession of Controlled Substance With Intent to Distribute, other VCITs produced large Racketeer Influenced and Corrupt Organization Act (RICO) indictments involving multiple individuals.

When the Pittsburgh VCIT team started in June 2004, one of the main focuses was to conduct a public campaign to apprehend ATF wanted persons. In coordination with the United States Attorney's Office for the Western District of Pennsylvania, VCIT quickly obtained approximately 20 Federal firearms-related indictments of ATF wanted persons in Pittsburgh. The resulting warrants were executed and provided necessary momentum to the VCIT strategy. The VCIT anticipated early in the pilot period that a collateral benefit to this strategy would be developing a variety of confidential informants (CI). However, the severity of charges lodged against offenders often resulted in their detention pending trial. While this prevented them from gathering timely street intelligence, it did result in defendants who provided important historical information as a result of plea negotiations. CIs capable of providing necessary street level intelligence, the basis of proactive investigations, were developed using alternative means.

BEST PRACTICE # 4: Use the full array of intelligence resources.

Using a complement of ATF and local intelligence is critical to the foundation of any VCIT strategy. The ATF Tucson Field Office, in conjunction with the Tucson Police Department and the Arizona Criminal Justice Commission, synthesized data from gun traces provided by ATF's National Tracing Center, along with local violent crime reports to identify geographic hot-spots requiring VCIT intervention.

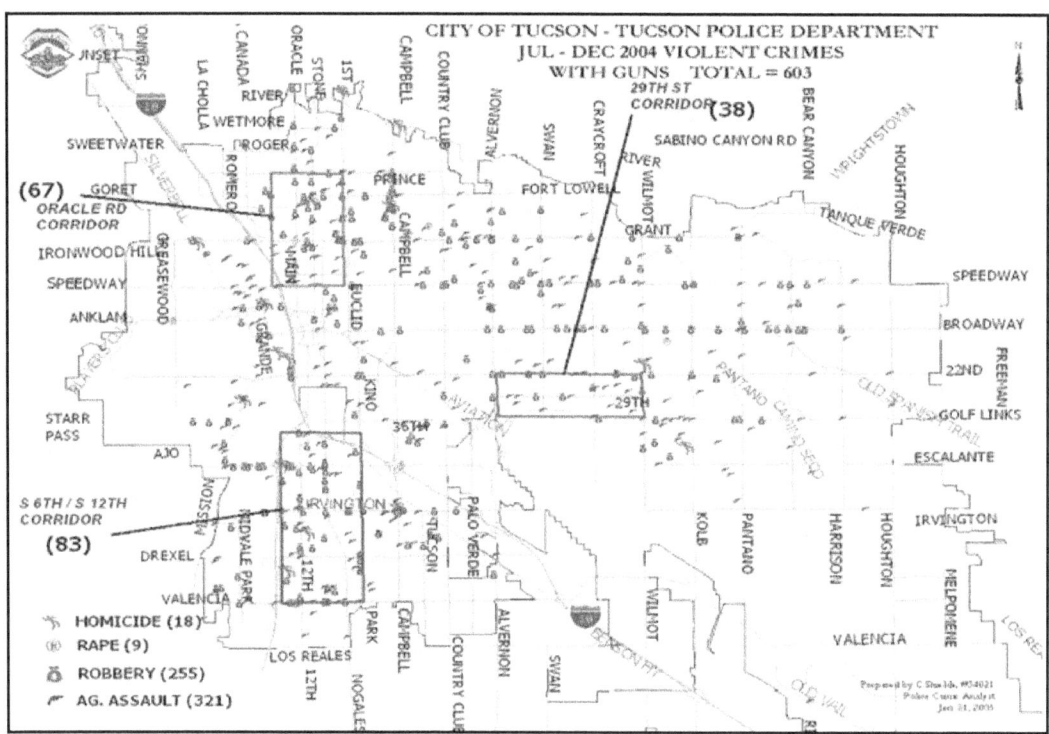

Detailed mapping of firearms trace results along with detailed mapping of areas within the city where crimes were being committed with firearms was key to success.

Partnering together, the Tucson VCIT devised and implemented a 3-prong enforcement strategy that included a Firearms Trafficking Initiative, a proactive Street Enforcement Initiative, and a targeted Repeat Offender Initiative.

In furtherance of the Firearms Trafficking Initiative, team members use firearms trace data and information provided by the Tucson Police Department (TPD) analyst, ATF Tucson Field Office support staff, and partnerships with local firearms dealers to identify and prosecute the sources of firearms to the criminal element. As part of the Street Enforcement Initiative, the team assesses all firearms offenses originating in three target areas and responds jointly to conduct significant investigations and make arrests of firearms offenders. Under the Repeat Offender Initiative, ATF, the Tucson police, the United States Probation Office, and the Arizona Board of Parole and Probation worked together to arrest repeat offenders when they were caught in possession of firearms or ammunition. These "worst of the worst" offenders are identified in the Tucson police computer system with orders to contact VCIT members if these individuals are found in possession of firearms. This initiative has resulted in the arrest of several armed felons, preventing further acts of violence.

BEST PRACTICE # 5: Maintain a fluid and dynamic approach when targeting offenders and hot spots of violent crime.

While addressing the complex crime problems found in metropolitan cities, VCITs found that a fluid and dynamic approach to targeting offenders and identifying hot spots for crime was required. The Los Angeles VCIT focused its investigative and enforcement efforts in both the City and County of Los Angeles, targeting gang members, parolees, and others identified as responsible for firearms-related crimes and other crimes of violence. These areas fell within the local jurisdiction of the Los Angeles Police Department and the Los Angeles County Sheriff's Department. Based on an historical analysis of violent and gun crime, VCIT members identified two areas that initially warranted the greatest attention. Despite a heavy police presence, both areas were plagued by violent street gang activity, homicides, assaults, and shootings. Additionally, an emerging trend among Los Angeles gang members requiring immediate attention was unprovoked shootings at police officers. However, during the implementation phase of the Los Angeles VCIT strategy, ATF learned that other divisions of Los Angeles and the neighboring Montebello Police Department faced similar problems with gang members and others perpetrators of violent crime. This required the VCIT to expand the scope of its initial strategy. As a result, the LA VCIT chose to operate full time in the Southeast and Rampart Divisions. On a case-by-case basis the team conducted operations in the Pacific and Southwest Divisions, and in the City of Montebello where Rampart gang members maintained community ties.

BEST PRACTICE # 6: Conduct proactive street enforcement with local police in targeted hot spots.

VCITs conducting proactive street enforcement in targeted areas contributed to significant declines in firearms-related crime and homicides. ATF's Philadelphia Field Division decided to employ the VCIT as part of an integrated firearms reduction strategy. The VCIT aggressively investigated all shootings in the target areas, leading to the apprehension of suspects before possible future homicides could occur. Simultaneously, three additional ATF groups separately perfected investigations as a part of Project Safe Neighborhoods task force, a firearms trafficking group, and a group dedicated to perfecting long-term conspiracy and RICO-type cases. In cities that do not have the resources to dedicate entire groups to such a strategy, tough choices are required. One VCIT experienced an increase in homicides over the pilot period in their area of operations while dedicating significant resources to a long-term operation targeting a single organization. A proactive street enforcement approach may provide more positive results.

VCITs found that partnerships with patrol units are true force multipliers compared to similar relationships with detective bureaus. Such collaborative, interjurisdictional teams promoted better intelligence sharing and problem solving, and have raised the effectiveness of Federal law enforcement officers and patrol officers alike.

Federal special agents gained from the experience of operating as cases unfolded, as opposed to leading historical investigations involving offenses that occurred weeks, if not months, before. Real time activity enabled law enforcement to stop criminals and disarm shooters immediately.

Targeting high crime hot spots and working the streets with local police are enforcement strategies that work. Greensboro, North Carolina, VCIT members partnered with Greensboro Police Department (GPD) for greater ATF/Federal visibility in the community and with the criminal element. The VCIT assigned an agent to partner with the GPD "T-Set" (tactical street enforcement teams) each night of the week. Suspects who encountered ATF agents voiced concerns over potential Federal prosecution. Homicides in Greensboro dropped from 39 in 2003 to 16 in 2004. During the VCIT pilot program, homicides with firearms dropped from 13 in 2003 to 3 during the same 6-month period in 2004.

BEST PRACTICE # 7: Deploy resources during peak hours of criminal activity.

Shift scheduling is critical to task force performance. Close monitoring of crime data and benchmarking efforts by other law enforcement agencies can empower team leaders to choose appropriate shifts and justify benefits to team members and supervisors alike.

Police operations during peak hours of criminal activity made VCITs more effective.

During the initial phase of the VCIT efforts in Pittsburgh, ATF agents and Pittsburgh Bureau of Police (PBP) detectives focused the street-level team efforts within the most violent neighborhoods within specific PBP Zones. These efforts consisted of vehicular surveillances, Terry stops, and direct VCIT response to PBP radio calls for assistance. These activities were conducted primarily during the height of criminal activity from 10:00 pm to 3:00 am. When the initiative began, there was an abundance of street violence and drug activity occurring on specific corners. After approximately 1 month of an increased presence on the street, violence that was on the rise began to fall.

Accordingly, as the violent criminals learned of the focused attention and VCIT's presence on the streets, overt criminal activity during the same hours became increasingly more difficult to locate. Additionally, the VCIT team members saw a shift in behavior concerning the concealment locations of criminally possessed firearms. More firearms were now being recovered from concealment locations in vehicles rather than on one's person. The PBP Command Staff directly attributed the aforementioned changes in behavior to the increased focus by VCIT on the street in combination with the threat of Federal prosecution.

BEST PRACTICE, # 8: Investigate the sources of firearms linked to violent crime.

Pittsburgh's VCIT, knowing the importance of investigating the sources of firearms linked to violent crime, initiated a notification protocol. When the VCIT initiative began, ATF requested that the police department provide immediate notification of all commercial and residential firearms thefts. As a result, VCIT responded to the theft scenes and conducted the investigation of numerous firearms burglaries with the PBP. This effort proved very productive, often leading to the recovery of all firearms from certain thefts. These efforts also netted many notorious burglars and drug abusers who were sources of stolen firearms to the streets.

Prosecutors partnered with the VCIT from the initial targeting of the worst offenders through prosecution.

BEST PRACTICE # 9: Prioritize prosecution of defendants linked to targeted hot spots.

A measured, balanced strategy, including a corresponding prosecutorial commitment to complement the law enforcement activity, was a cornerstone to the success seen in the program. Corresponding increases in prosecutorial resources are necessary to realize the full potential of the VCIT initiative. Focused prosecution efforts on firearms cases in the targeted areas generated tremendous momentum towards positively impacting violent firearms crimes. The positive momentum created by the United States Attorneys Offices (USAO) in prosecuting additional firearms cases requires a corresponding dedication of additional ATF resources to VCIT cities, as well as diligence in working with Federal and local prosecutors in screening and prioritizing those cases being prosecuted federally.

Many of the VCITs built upon existing collaborative partnerships established under Project Safe Neighborhoods. For example, the Miami-Dade States Attorney's Office (SAO) and USAO continued to actively support both the VCIT and Project Safe Neighborhoods initiatives in the review of firearm-related arrest cases. The inclusion of the prosecutorial resources throughout the process was important to the success in Miami. The SAO had collected the required data needed for geographic targeting for the VCIT initiative, playing an integral role from the project inception. The SAO had historically taken a lead role in the screening of state firearms arrests by assisting the USAO and

ATF in coordinating Federal, State, and local agencies in a unified offensive to combat gun violence. Through the collaborative efforts of ATF, the SAO, and the USAO, a decision was made on each violent crime involving a firearm as to the most appropriate venue for prosecution. This relationship was instrumental in impacting the firearms related homicides in Miami.

BEST PRACTICE # 10: Publicize success stories.

Publicizing success deters would be offenders, reduces fear in the community, and bolsters team morale of those working with VCIT teams. The Los Angeles VCIT found that highlighting ATF's work with local officers on the streets, grabbed the attention of the local gang members and related offenders. The word quickly spread that if ATF was involved, and arrests made, criminals were facing hard time in the Federal system.

The VCIT relayed timely information to the media to deter offenders and reduce fear in communities.

At the end of the project's pilot period, the VCIT supervisor assessed that more media exposure on the accomplishments of the VCIT would further its success. In particular, news releases on the status and significant prison sentences gang members and other violent offenders were receiving as a result of the VCIT's efforts would had a substantial impact on the streets. The message that "gun crime means hard time" is understood and taken seriously by the criminal element.

Additional Recommendations

While the previously mentioned Best Practices are understood to have the greatest impact on the success of VCIT initiatives, other actions will improve this Federal/Local partnership.

Each VCIT would benefit by addressing the following issues:

- Greater initial momentum could be created by formalizing Memorandums of Agreement (MOA) for State and local overtime reimbursements prior to the start of the program. Resolution of these issues would allow greater participation on the part of these departments, as the question of overtime reimbursement is always a topic of discussion.

- VCITs would benefit from having all participating officers, deputies, and detectives complete the "deputation" process prior to the program's initiation, allowing greater involvement on the part of State and local partners in the administrative and investigative report writing responsibilities of the team.

- Total commitment, support, and consistency from all involved United States Attorneys' Offices and District Attorney's Offices are key to the judicial success of the VCIT initiative. Without the threat of leveraging substantial Federal time against arrested gang members and other violent offenders, VCIT carries very little weight with ATF's State and local law enforcement counterparts, or with those responsible for the violent crime. (Seeing and hearing that ATF is working in concert on the streets with local law enforcement got the attention of the local gang members and related offenders. The word quickly spread that if Federal agents were involved and arrests made, offenders were facing hard time in the Federal system.)

- Additional laptop computers should be available for use by local officers and deputies, along with instructions on N-Force (ATF's case management system) and related investigative procedures.

- Annual VCIT manager's conferences should be held to communicate mission goals and reporting requirements. The conferences would bring task force members together, including ATF personnel and corresponding commanding officers from local police departments, as well as representatives from the United States Attorneys' offices and other represented agencies on the task force. This would provide VCIT leaders the opportunity to ask questions and conduct problem solving sessions. Once all leaders are unified in their understanding of the goals of VCIT and administrative requirements critical to performance measurement, the program can be implemented with greater efficiencey.

Successful Investigations

ALBUQUERQUE VCIT Recovers 41 Pipe Bombs: In Albuquerque, an undercover Albuquerque VCIT member purchased 41 pipe bombs from a suspect on three occasions. The first purchase netted four pipe bombs, the second yielded 17 pipe bombs, and the final buy/bust led to the recovery of 22 more.

BALTIMORE VCIT arrests Violent Felon on Parole: Baltimore VCIT members executed a Federal search warrant at the residence of one of the most violent felons in the Baltimore area. The suspect was a career criminal with previous convictions for robbery with a deadly weapon, possession with intent to manufacture and distribute narcotics, use of a handgun in a crime of violence, as well as other offenses. Officers obtained probable cause to believe that the subject purchased and possessed ammunition. Upon execution of a Federal search warrant, officers recovered ammunition and a bulletproof vest. This "worst of the worst" offender admitted to the purchase and possession of the prohibited items and pled guilty to Federal offenses resulting in a 15-year prison sentence.

CHATTANOOGA VCIT Long Term Operation Results In 12 Suspects Arrested: Members of the VCIT, including United States Marshals Service and the Chattanooga Police Department executed 15 arrests and five search warrants emanating from a 5-month long undercover operation. The operation resulted in the undercover purchase of narcotics and 39 firearms including several with obliterated serial numbers. Execution of the warrants resulted in the arrest of 12 suspects. The remaining three wanted persons have since been arrested. Narcotics and a firearm were seized during the execution of the warrants. Six of the suspects arrested were identified as the VCIT "worst of the worst" serious offenders.

COLUMBUS VCIT Conducts Roundup Of Violent Drug Traffickers: ATF, the Columbus Division of Police (CPD), Adult Parole Authority, United States Marshals Service, the Franklin County Sheriff's Office, and the Bureau of Criminal Identification and Investigation have conducted lengthy investigations of violent street level firearms and narcotics traffickers in the 10th and 19th precincts, and parts of the 11th and 12th precincts of Columbus, Ohio.

Columbus VCIT questions a targeted offender.

The Columbus Police Department supports a VCIT roundup.

Agents and officers conducted a roundup of 70 suspects that were indicted by a Federal grand jury based upon undercover buys. All of these individuals are facing substantial federal jail time in relation to these narcotics and weapons-related charges. Most are exposed to at least 5 years minimum mandatory time and some are looking at life in jail. This operation will have a large impact on crime in this tight knit community that will continue into the future.

Another prong of the VCIT approach was a collaborative effort with the Special Response Bureau and the Patrol Section of the Columbus Division of Police. The VCIT initiative resulted in the arrest of 465 individuals for narcotics and weapons related charges. Sixty-three fugitives were arrested and 443 weapons were recovered. Approximately 5,000 grams of crack cocaine, 90,000 grams of marijuana and more than $23,000 were seized during this same period. Nine individuals who were identified as the "worst of the worst" were arrested from a list that was compiled at the onset of the VCIT initiative.

GREENSBORO VCIT Obtains Guilty Verdict Of "Worst Of The Worst" from VCIT Targeted List: An individual with multiple felony convictions, identified as one of the "worst of the worst" by the VCIT, was found guilty in an eight-count Federal indictment. The charges included possession of a firearm by a felon and other Federal firearms and narcotics violations. His past criminal history qualifies him as a career offender and he is facing 360 months in Federal prison. He was ranked number two on Greensboro's VCIT targeted list.

LAS VEGAS VCIT Recovers Homemade Machineguns: In Las Vegas, a man who authorities had been investigating since 1996, was finally taken off the streets when VCIT members conducted controlled purchases of homemade machineguns. These buys led to the recovery of 15 homemade machineguns from his residence.

LOS ANGELES VCIT Arrests Armed Drug Traffickers In Rampart: In August 2004, the Los Angeles VCIT and the Los Angeles Police Department Rampart Narcotics unit conducted a State search warrant in a VCIT target area. As a result of the search, two individuals were arrested for possession and trafficking of narcotics. Two kilograms of cocaine powder, a gallon plastic bag filled with rock cocaine, approximately 1 pound of black tar heroin, and 3 handguns (a Lorcin, a Taurus, and a Ruger) were seized from the location. Members of the VCIT took the suspects into custody. Both defendants are believed to be members or associates of the Diamond Street Gang that operates in the Rampart area and both are illegal immigrants.

Photographs courtesy of Corbis Corporation

MIAMI VCIT Executes Federal Arrest And Search Warrants In An International Arms Trafficking Investigation: In August 2004, special agents from ATF VCIT, Bureau of Immigration and Customs Enforcement, and the Miami Dade Police Department executed Federal arrest and search warrants in an ongoing international firearms trafficking and VCIT case.

This case has exposed a corrupt Federal firearms licensee who had been trafficking firearms and ammunition in container loads of used appliances to Venezuela for the past 7 or 8 years.

- Six of seven targets have pled guilty as charged; the seventh remains a fugitive in China.
- Items seized included:
  - 233 firearms including 26 machineguns and 42 firearms with obliterated serial numbers;
  - 50 AR-15 Drop In Auto Sears; approximately 691,000 rounds of ammunition; firearms parts for the conversion of firearms to fully automatic fire; and $5,684 in cash.

MIAMI VCIT Uses NIBIN to Help Solve Crimes: In October 2004, the Miami-Dade Police Department Crime Laboratory used the NIBIN system to link 9mm casings recovered at a carjacking, armed robbery and two other shootings over a 6-month period, leading to the identification and arrest of a suspect confirmed by victims of the shootings.

PHILADELPHIA VCIT Leverages Federal Charges To Arrest "Worst Of The Worst": In June 2004, the Philadelphia VCIT arrested a "Worst of the Worst" violent offender. The violent offender fought VCIT members, requiring the use of a taser by law enforcement. Subsequent to the search warrant, five handguns, including an assault pistol, a pistol with an obliterated serial number, and a bulletproof vest were seized, as well as other evidence. The assault pistol seized was linked through ballistic analysis to shell casings recovered from an incident involving the target in which an innocent bystander was shot. The target was a reputed armed robber and shooter, with an extensive arrest history, including an arrest for murder. He was released from State custody after posting bail. Upon release from custody, Philadelphia VCIT arrested the target on a complaint warrant charging him with Possession of a Firearm with an Obliterated Serial Number related to one of the firearms previously seized. Once again, upon his arrest by the Philadelphia VCIT, the suspect was armed with a handgun and fought VCIT members, requiring the use of a taser by law enforcement. The target was found guilty by jury of one count of Possession of a Firearm with an Obliterated Serial Number and is being held pending sentencing.

Firearms with obliterated serial numbers were key evidence used against targeted offenders.

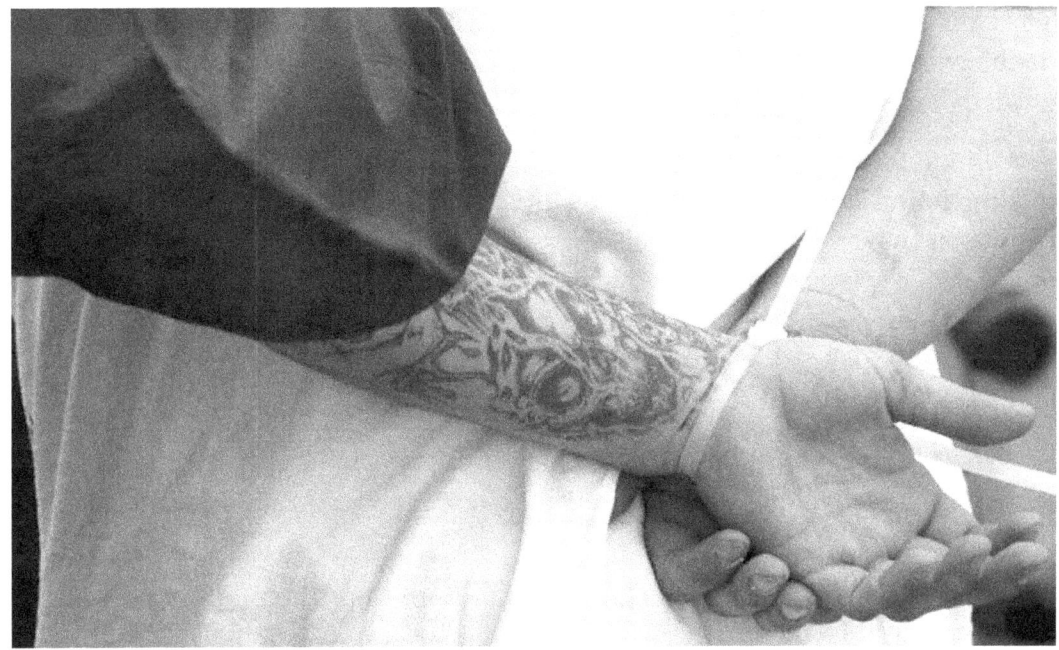
Gangs were linked to firearms-related violence in 13 of 15 VCIT cities.

PITTSBURGH VCIT Arrests Gun Trafficker And Recovers Firearms:
VCIT investigators developed information regarding a scheme in which
firearms were being trafficked into a VCIT target area of Pittsburgh. This
straw purchasing scheme involved a suspected firearms trafficker offering
heroin to individuals who would purchase firearms for him. The trafficker was
then selling these firearms in a VCIT target area of Pittsburgh. The target was
arrested on firearms charges, which carry a mandatory minimum sentence of
5 years, and one of the straw purchased firearms and narcotics were seized.
Charges are pending against the straw purchaser, Pittsburgh VCIT recovered
five firearms that had been illegally sold within the VCIT target area.

RICHMOND VCIT Conducts Gun Show Operation: In October 2004, The
Richmond VCIT conducted an enforcement operation at the Richmond gun
show. The operation included 45 law enforcement personnel from ATF, the
Richmond Police Department and the Virginia State Police. The enforcement
activity resulted in the seizure of 15 firearms from 24 individuals. Charges
against six of these individuals are pending, while others have been identified
as witnesses. Those being charged include a known drug dealer, a juvenile who
had stolen a firearm, and a number of convicted felons (including a convicted
murderer) who were attempting to use straw purchasers to illegally obtain
firearms.

TAMPA VCIT Arrests Home Invasion Suspects: In July 2004, a Tampa
Police Department Confidential Informant provided information to ATF
concerning home invasions and other criminal activity in the Tampa, area.

Through a series of controlled telephone calls and meetings with an ATF undercover agent, plans were finalized for the commission of a robbery of an alleged narcotics stash house.

The Tampa VCIT arrested three suspects following an undercover meeting relating to this home invasion investigation. At the time of the arrest, Officers recovered firearms, narcotics and other equipment intended for use in the home invasion. The vehicle driven by the targets was reported stolen the morning of the arrest. One of the targets is currently a suspect in a homicide investigation.

TUCSON VCIT Seizes Firearms Cache: In October 2004, while servicing several Federal search warrants at two Tucson residences, the Tucson VCIT seized 20 AK-47 rifles and five 100-round drum magazines and arrested three suspects, including one who had straw purchased the recovered firearms and 11 others earlier that month.

TULSA VCIT Arrests Major Gang Leader And Significant Seizure: In June 2004, Tulsa VCIT activities included numerous arrests following a wiretap of a major Tulsa gang leader. The value of the National Integrated Ballistic Information Network (NIBIN) became readily apparent during this project when a backlog of entries of gang-related shootings was remedied with ATF support. As soon as this backlog was taken care of, the Tulsa police department began having a number of hits linking several previously unrelated shootings. The information from the hits proved invaluable to the VCIT effort in that it linked several shootings to identified gang members, thus further documenting their their involvement in the aggravated violence in the area. Also in June, 2004, during the execution of a joint ATF and Tulsa Police Department search warrant at three locations, agents and officers recovered firearms, 3 kilograms of cocaine, and more than $500,000.

WASHINGTON DC/NORTHERN VIRGINIA VCIT Arrests Firearms Trafficker: In June 2004, a confidential informant introduced an ATF undercover agent to a suspect who stated he could supply large amounts of firearms and narcotics. The suspect traveled from southern Virginia to Washington D.C. and sold the undercover agent 10 handguns and 1 pound of marijuana. ATF agents arrested the suspect in September 2004 and are now following up on the sources of the trafficked firearms.

ATF Commitment

To address the problem of violent crime, Federal, State, and local law enforcement agencies recognize that recent technological and investigative advances have empowered law enforcement to impact the criminal element in a community like never before. Our Federal, State, and local partners must have a working knowledge of ATF capabilities available to them in support of their local enforcement efforts. ATF is committed to distributing new technologies to help suppress violent criminals in VCIT cities. Collectively, these tools enhance the ability to collect, analyze, and disseminate data and thereby increase the potential for identifying violent crime areas, targeting those individuals responsible for firearms-related crime and other crimes of violence, and improving the quality of life in these communities.

The following is a list of technologies and a description of their supporting programs. Many of these tools are utilized to accomplish the goals of the VCIT initiative.

National Integrated Ballistic Information Network (NIBIN)

ATF's NIBIN program provides advanced investigative support to State and local law enforcement in combating firearms-related violent crimes and serial shooting incidents. NIBIN provided focused investigative assistance to VCIT cities through the integration of various violence reduction programs and new forensic technology. The system utilizes computerized imaging systems, along with investigative support to improve the efficiency of the examination of ballistic evidence. The Integrated Ballistic Identification System (IBIS) is a single platform computer identification system, that correlates and matches both projectile and shell casing ballistic evidence. The benefit of these comparisons is the ability to link ballistic evidence, giving law enforcement another tool to confirm links in related shootings.

Regional Crime Gun Centers

ATF's four regional crime gun centers provide support for ATF, as well as support other Federal, State and local law enforcement agencies to reduce violent crime within their regions. These centers have the technology to collect, analyze and disseminate intelligence information derived from various sources. They also provide visual representation of information obtained from ATF's Firearms Tracing System (FTS), Geographic Information System (GIS) mapping of firearms data to identify hot spots of criminal activity and the sources of illegal firearms.

Crime Gun Analysis Branch (CGAB)

The CGAB provides support for ATF and other Federal, State and local law enforcement agencies nationwide to reduce violent crime. The CGAB has the technology to provide visual representations of information obtained from ATF's FTS and GIS to identify hot spots of criminal activity and the sources illegal firearms on the national level.

They analyze data on guns used in crimes collected by ATF and other law enforcement agencies; identify illegal firearms traffickers who supply arms to criminals; transmit investigative leads; create analytical tools for use by law enforcement; and develop partnerships with the academic community for joint analytical projects regarding crime gun data.

The information gathered from the four regional crime gun centers and CGAB provide law enforcement with specific intelligence through firearms tracing and GIS mapping of areas within a city that have a high violent crime rate involving gangs and illegal use and possession of firearms. The systems assist in identifying areas of heavy firearms activity, allowing law enforcement to focus additional resources to combat violent firearms activities in identified areas.

National Tracing Center (NTC)

ATF's NTC is the only facility/operation in the world that traces the history of firearms recovered in crimes and from juveniles for any Federal, State, or local law enforcement agency in the United States or abroad. The NTC traces firearms involved in crimes to the individuals who purchased the weapon, linking suspects to crimes. The NTC provides around the-clock assistance to Federal, State, local and international law

enforcement agencies to aid in their fight against firearms-related violent crimes. The NTC maintains information concerning the multiple sales of firearms, suspect guns, stolen firearms, and firearms with obliterated serial numbers, and is also the only repository for all out-of-business records of Federal firearms licensees.

The intelligence gathered from the tracing of firearms assists in developing leads of those involved in violent crime. ATF utilizes Online LEAD, one of many databases that NTC maintains, as a primary tool to develop illegal firearms trafficking leads involving gang members and their associates. Online LEAD provides investigators with data on gun activity involving gangs, such as types of guns most frequently used by gang members, areas where gang members' guns were being recovered, and individuals who purchase guns for gang members.

National Laboratory Center

ATF's laboratory system is composed of the National Laboratory Center (NLC) in Ammendale, Maryland, and the regional laboratories in Atlanta, Georgia, and San Francisco, California. These laboratories are recognized as the leaders in the field of firearms, and are at the cutting edge of firearms scientific techniques.

National Field Office Case Information System (NFOCIS)

NFOCIS provides an integrated and centralized data management solution that allows for real time monitoring and oversight of all law enforcement and industry operations activities in the field, as well as all investigative matters of the divisions. NFOCIS provides a platform for analysis of case information to aid in the identification and tracking of violent criminals and provides the ability to coordinate and execute arrest/search warrants of violent criminals targeted in the various strategies.

Canine Operations Branch

Explosives detection canines, primarily trained and used for identifying possible explosive devices, have evolved into an integral part of firearms investigations through their ability to locate hidden firearms and ammunition. The newfound use is especially valuable during search warrants and following shootings when other means of locating firearms, ammunition, and shell casings are unsuccessful.

Conclusion

The initial pilot of the VCIT program was an enormous success. Teams contributed to significant reductions in targeted crimes in 13 of 15 cities. The program worked because of strong relationships between Federal partners such as DEA, FBI and the U.S. Marshals Service, along with the local agencies that serve as the foundation of the program. The dedicated efforts and hard work of the task force members, their innovative ideas, and community involvement made communities safer, and saved lives. Teams that conducted proactive street operations, rather than simply responding after the fact to the enforcement efforts of others, made the greatest impact.

The documented success of the pilot program led to its implementation in five additional cities in fiscal year 2005. As announced by Attorney General Alberto Gonzales, the five cities include Camden, New Jersey; Fresno, California; Hartford, Connecticut; Houston, Texas; and New Orleans, Louisiana. Success of the program in the future will depend on maintaining the momentum and learning the lessons taught by deployment of the program.

VCIT was designed to be measurable. Its design and the reporting of critical data spoke to the VCIT's effectiveness nationwide. ATF field assets were empowered to devise individual strategies with law enforcement partners to prevent violent crimes committed with guns and were held accountable for localized results. The key to achieving future goals hinges on the ability of each city to analyze its unique problems and develop its solutions capitalizing on the unique expertise of every partner. Continued accountability and providing appropriate resources to the field to fund aggressive and targeted enforcement efforts will be required to maintain the momentum of this unique enforcement program.

ATF

Bureau of Alcohol, Tobacco,
Firearms and Explosives

For further information regarding the Violent Crime
Impact Team program, contact:

U.S. Department of Justice
Bureau of Alcohol, Tobacco, Firearms and Explosives
Office of Enforcement Programs and Services
Firearms Enforcement Branch
(202) 927-7770

ATF Publication 3501.1
Revised December 2005